Stephen ROCHE

Noël Truyers

In the **footsteps** of **Eddy** Merckx

Stephen Roche had already gained enormous popularity which, underlined by his black curls and irresistible smile, needed nothing more than a few major results to see it explode. It was a peak that he was to enjoy during a fabulous campaign in 1987.

That year, the son of a humble Dublin milk man, took his place amongst the all-time greats. Betrayed by bad luck in Paris-Nice, Roche gave his all to finish fourth in Liège-Bastogne-Liège, Flèche Wallonne and in the Grand Prix of Frankfurt before pulling off an historic triple: a gutsy victory in the Giro d'Italia, despite a virtual mutiny from his team-mates (for having driven Roberto Visentini to defeat, he was severely attacked by all of Italy); victory in the Tour de France thanks to a refreshing cocktail of class and aggression; and a brilliant world title win at Villach in Austria.

At 27, Roche became the second person in cycling history to claim the triple in the same year. The only one to have done it before was Eddy Merckx.

At the end of September, 1987 Ireland welcomed Roche back home like a hero. Dublin placed him on the mantle as a

Citizen of honour in Dublin. *(Photo: Graham Watson)*

citizen of honour, giving him the keys to the city. It was a privilege only shared with former US President J.F Kennedy; the Emperor of Japan, Akihito; Pope Jean-Paul II and Nelson Mandela. Early in the morning, workers managed to erect a giant tribune in front of the Bank of Ireland. Under the eyes of all the dignitaries dressed in blue robes, two footmen carried a golden sword and a sceptre laden with gems and climbed the steps ahead of Roche. At his side was Carmencita Hederman, the Mayor of Dublin, who was going to make him the citizen of honour of his city.

"A lot of young Irish people are being inspired by your example. You've known how to make use of your talents in the best way possible. In holding onto the belief that the impossible is at the door for those who want it, you have been able to inspire all those around you. Your devotion, your self-sacrifice has been understood by all Irish people - young and not so young - that we can still conquer the world," she declared solemnly while seizing hold of the sceptre.

Stephen Roche became the 58th citizen of honour to be awarded the prestigious Honorary Freedom of the City of Dublin. Several weeks after the celebrations, Roche's dream became a nightmare: his knee once again causing him great pain. Incapable of rediscovering his best form, the world champion once more fell into anonymity.

With his wife Lydia and the yellow jersey of the Tour.
(Photo: Graham Watson)

He started to come out of it again at the beginning of 1989, yet without ever showing the form he had before. During the next six years he won one more stage in Paris-Nice, the Four Days of Dunkirk, the Catalan Week, the Criterium International and an unforgettable stage to La Bourbole in the 1992 Tour de France under a blanket of fog and euphoria. It was his very last triumph before bringing a discrete end to his career. At the end of 1993, the Irishman bade farewell to the peloton for good.

A triumphant passage through Dublin.   *(Photo: Graham Watson)*

Euphoric times

By 1998 Stephen Roche had survived 38 springs. During this time he had experienced some euphoric times as well as some gut wrenching moments. With his wife Lydia and their two children, Nicolas and Christelle, he moved to a house perched high above of the ring roads of Dublin.

The Roche household is surrounded by flowers and plants which liven up the vast lawns surrounding it. "You see those houses at the end and to the right?," asks Roche while parking his car. "It's the millionaires' quarter where Damon Hill lives, as well as Eddy Irvine, Bono from U2, Chris Rea and Phil Collins. There are some really nice houses there where everything is really planned: the swimming pool, grass watering system. It's different here," he says with a relaxed air.

A lead mine

Roche's eyes are always sparkling with cheeky youth, characteristic of his times as a rider. He always kept his irreverent side. His cheeks have been rounded by time and his lips thickened, but this hasn't really altered his playful character, nor his natural tendency to leave people guessing.

He still loves to chat or recount stories, and opens his heart to others. "Life over there is good. I also had a house in that area, but we sold it to build one here. I prefer to admire the countryside from the other side high up, near the towers. What you'll notice here is that there is still an old lead mine.

"It's still possible to go down into the mine shafts. A long time ago, many miners earned their living there. It's on the steep climb to the entry of the mine that I learned how to climb on a bike. I had to go up it hundreds and hundreds of times. I left litres of sweat on this brute of a climb. It took nearly an hour to haul myself to the top, and it really hurt my legs. We used to carry a little oil lamp, gather some dead wood, light a match and then grill some sausages. Then at nightfall, we took our bikes and plummeted down the descent at top speed to get back home."

In front of his house in the suburbs of Paris.
(Photo: Rug)

The **exile**

Stephen Roche gets back behind the steering wheel of his four wheel drive car, closes the door, and gets ready to go back down the hill. "Being Irish, it would seem normal that I should live in Ireland. But it's not so simple. My wife is French. At home we speak French and the children go to a French school. On Mondays they take lessons to improve their English. We don't wish to live in France any longer. At the start we thought about moving to Italy. I had the chance to work in public relations for Carrera, but the house was 18km from my children's school: too far for the children. It was Lydia who chose to live in Dublin. Obviously I was very happy about that. After all, Dublin is my birthplace."

Like Sean Kelly, Roche enjoyed his time of glory in Paris-Nice. *(Photo: Graham Watson)*

Below: A warrior's rest. *(Photo: Noël Truyers)*

Nicolas

Under the sun the view is magnificent. Roche approaches the traffics lights. "Most people think that it rains all the time in Ireland. You can see that that's not true. I love this country. I remember the world championships that we disputed, Sean Kelly and I. When we put on our Irish jerseys, we were so proud. We never raced to be the first Irishman, but to make sure our national jersey was always at the front line of action. I feel happy here and we are all starting to really feel at home. The children too. Our daughter Christelle is 12, and she plays the piano, swims, does gymnastics and dances. Nicolas is 14, and cycles. "He's a bit like me at that age: not really good, but he likes it. Last year he finished fourth in the Irish championship. He won one race, a time trial. He also plays football. I let him do it without

Stephen - master of the house. (Photo: Noël Truyers)

putting pressure on him, just as happened to me at the time."

Simplicity

Before he returned to his homeland, Roche lived in Sagy-Seillancourt, a small country suburb about 30 kilometres from Paris. There weren't any shops or cafés. Just a telephone cabin lost in the huge expanse of green pastures. By passing on something with more than two wheels, we missed the village.

Peace and quiet guaranteed, Roche lives in a house surrounded by a wall through which we passed by two automatic gates equipped with CCTV. In his garage, he has four cars, two of which are classics. It's his hobby.

Roche had the success and the financial security which allow him to live comfortably, but he has always preferred a simple life. We visited him several years

ago at home. He served coffee and biscuits without any formality. While carrying out his duty as host, he was surprised by his wife's request to ask him to pass by the butcher's. "Tonight there will be steak on the menu."

Private life

Roche has always regarded his private life as important. "It was often difficult to preserve it totally when I was a rider. I remember the winter of 1987, after my wins in the Giro d'Italia, Tour de France and the world titles. The night before Christmas Eve an Italian television crew came to our place, pretending to have had the okay from Patrick Valcke, my directeur-sportif. After the incident, I learned that Pat had passed on my address to them. They invaded the living room with all their gear and asked me if it was okay, to help report, to unwrap the chrildrens' Christmas presents two days earlier. Of course, I refused. My children are sacred."

France

Between Roche and France there is a love story that will last forever. "I owe everything to the country; sporting-wise first as it is there where I claimed my greatest wins; then, of course, on the private side of things. I remember exactly the day I went to the Continent. I wanted to become a cyclist and I knew that to become one I had to leave Ireland where the level of racing was insufficient. So, I packed my bags with my heart full of anxiety. I was lucky that it all worked out for the best. I discovered people who are exceptionally friendly. Then I met Lydia, my wife."

Lightning bolt

It's an episode which André Arnaud, Roche's father-in-law, remembers as if it happened yesterday. "It was the spring of 1979. There was an amateur race in the region. All the family, all the supporters, went there with my elder brother, Michel, to cheer him on. In the ACBB team, considered as the breeding ground for the prestigious Peugeot team, there was a small frail-looking boy, an Irishman called Roche. As soon as Lydia saw him, it was like a lightning bolt had struck," recalls André, mimicking his son-in-law.

"Our looks crossed many times," adds Roche. "My heart beat like mad, and I suppose that Lydia's also beat madly. She already had this smile that I could never resist."

Lydia, his wife, is French. (Photo: Noël Truyers)

Gratitude

Roche is the first to recognise the value of his beautiful family. "It's thanks to Lydia's parents that I was able to get where I did. As a new professional with Peugeot, I £500 a month, after tax. It was the reign of survival. My parents-in-law had a business in which the attic had been made into a little studio. It was there that I started. Lydia was only 18 when we married, but she immediately proved to be an excellent mistress of the house. Then the children came: first Nicolas, then Christelle two years later. Everything that happened to make my life evolved during my time in France, but deep down in my heart I always remained attached to Ireland. I was happy to hear the kids speak English. I installed a satellite antenna so they could hear and watch the cartoons on the BBC."

Time out for gardening. *(Photo: Noël Truyers)*

Black curly hair and full, round cheeks characterise his image.
(Caricature: Nesten)

The passion of **rally driving**

A passion for rally driving

Stephen Roche had just repainted his garage. He took advantage of that to put everything in order in his junk room and put everything neatly in place on shelves, and arranged all his bikes, wheels and tyres. On the wall a giant poster of him in the pink jersey of the Giro draws your attention. "It's a present given to me by a friend who drives a bus in Dublin. He made up this poster during the year of my victory in Italy and he put it up in his bus. The bus passengers who knew nothing about cycling could no longer live in ignorance."

Porsche

Two Harley Davidsons gleam with all their polish, clean as if brand new. They have replaced the rally cars which Roche had to get rid of. "At the time I couldn't stay in one place for more than an hour without going crazy. Rally driving was a consuming passion. I spent a little fortune on it. Sean Kelly has always been economical with his money, sharing his life between races and his home. Today, he drives a Mercedes, but at the time he drove around in a Citroen CX which had 300,000km on it. As I didn't smoke or drink, I bought myself a Porsche. It was an investment of sorts, but it was a little bit crazy too. I certainly wouldn't allow it today. I'm happy enough with something

more modest - a Jeep. As for rally driving, it's an old story."

Triumph

Let's go back to this passion which Roche even once thought of making a second career. "It was at the time when I was suffering from my knee problems that I came upon rally driving. Mentally, I needed to get out of the trough, to change my thoughts, to rid myself of stress by getting into a similar activity. Cycling takes so much out of you that sometimes you need to take yourself away from it so it won't destroy you. I have always been attracted by cars. When I was young I worked in a garage

Roche has always had a passion for old cars.
(Photo: Noël Truyers)

Crazy for speed. (Photo: Rug)

where I got the bug for old cars. The first that I bought was a Triumph TR6. I spent hours pulling it apart, to repair everything and then put it back together."

Fina

As a driver, Roche took part most notably in the Rally Condroz in Belgium as well as the Monaco Rally with the help of Opel. "We did it all very professionally. We had posters, personalised suits, a truck, a land cruiser, five mechanics who looked after the slightest of problems. There was nothing to envy the other teams for. At the time I was still cycling for the Histor-Sigma team, a Belgian paint manufacturer. I had told Mr Desmet - the boss of their affiliate, Petrofina - that we raced with Esso petrol. You can imagine his reaction. He immediately took it upon himself to negotiate with the team hierarchy, and finally we were using Fina petrol"

Concentration

Rally driving wasn't a past-time without risk for Roche. During the race at Condroz, the Irishman's car spun off the course. "What luck. It happened to us the season before for that matter. To be honest, I drove far too fast in relation to the limited experience I had. On top of that, I didn't go over the course beforehand. I took too many risks and we ended up against a tree. Everyone recognised that I had a certain amount of talent. At the time of the accident, we were 25th from 170 teams. Not bad, eh? Previously I even finished second in the Rally of Hainaut. I also took part in the Rally of Ireland. Okay, there are certain risks in this activity; but one is never really totally safe, no matter where you are. Greg LeMond nearly lost his life in a simple hunting trip. Rally driving has one similarity to cycling: concentration at every moment. I finished some rallies as mentally tired as in a long stage of the Tour de France."

First steps

At Dundrum, ten minutes outside Dublin, there's practically no traffic at all. Roche drives his Jeep every day through the streets of what is a modest area. "You see that football ground there? Well, for me, it was there where everything began. Like most of my mates at the time, I played football. But the lady who lived just in front of the stadium knew that I loved cycling."

At that precise moment that lady appeared on her front door step. It was a sign for Roche.

"She explained that she was starting a cycling club in the village, and that it would be great if I would become a member. That is how I became a Sunday rider. It was not the same with Sean Kelly who rode every day. Me, I preferred to go out on the bike in my area for fun, for simple pleasure. The idea of making a

career out of cycling hadn't yet crossed my mind. I only won now and then. No, putting it simply, I rode for pleasure, without pressure. The real ambition didn't come till later, and very slowly."

Newspaper

"It's true that at home cycling was a habit. My parents always rode a lot. That is how they first met," says Roche whose uncle also dabbled in competition, but without really making any major breakthrough. On the other hand, his grandfather, Ned, developed a solid reputation as a swimmer, a sport in which Roche wasn't too bad at either. However, it was towards cycling that the young Irishman really wanted to go. "At 13, I started racing with a bike that had large tyres. At home nobody knew anything; until they found

my name in the local paper. However, they immediately gave the okay for me to pursue it."

The milk run

Bonnie, Roche's mother, often described her little boy as an individualist. "He always carried out his plan alone, worked hard and never balked at giving someone a hand."

Roche smiles upon hearing this. "It's true. I never looked for an easy time. My father had a milk run and I went with him to help. I wanted to make sure I did my bit. To cycle cost quite a bit of money in those days and I needed to have the means to travel regularly to France. From six in the morning I was up and ready. My father drove the truck and I put the milk bottles on the door step of his clients. After that, I went to school. I got my plumbing diploma which allowed me to be employed by the Milk Department.

Night ferry

It was a job that one would think was totally out of place for a cyclist, but Roche still made do with it. "I was a maintenance worker in the dairy for which my father was a distributor. My job was to repair machines blocked by pieces of glass from broken bottles inside the machines. I often went home covered in oil and milk. The hours were tiring and the overtime was regular. Most often I went to the dairy on my bike and in the evening I managed to get in 40 or so kilometres of training. The

A young professional with Peugeot. (Photo: AP)

only positive point was the pay for overtime. Thanks to that I was able to pay for my ferry ticket to France to race there on the weekends. I would take the ferry back home on the Sunday night and then return to work on Monday morning."

ACBB

It was a lifestyle that Roche could not have supported for ever. He spent quite a bit of time trying to find a solution to this problem. "It came the day that I met Lucien Bailly, the president of ACBB Paris. His warning was frank and direct: if I didn't manage to discover a more regular lifestyle as soon as possible I could forget my plans of a professional career. Hence, I took leave without pay for six months and I was taken in by this famous cycling club. Phil Anderson had gone there, then Robert Millar. Alas, six months later, I hadn't really been convinced and I seriously thought about going home. "Hang in there,' Lucien Bailly told me. It will all change if you can just win a good race.' The next day, I won the amateur Paris-Roubaix; and from that I got my first professional contract with Peugeot."

A rosy life

Brother Laurence

Stephen Roche continues through the streets of Dundrum. In another quarter, he stops his Jeep in front of a charming little house. The garden is meticulously kept. Then there's the entrance path that Roche gladly knocked together just like that. This is here Roche's parents live. Upon our arrival, his father is busy mowing the lawn. This house is where Roche was born and grew up with his sisters Pamela and Carol, and brothers Jude and Lawrence. A two-year-old boy leaps happily around the house under the watchful eye of his grand mother, Bonnie. "It's the son of my brother Lawrence who was also a professional and even did the Tour de France. However, he never really had the chance to prove his potential in the professional peloton. In fact, he was a bit of a victim of his family name: we were always waiting for him to make a name for himself. It was a shame because he did have ability," says Roche. The two brothers are very much alike. The same eyes, the same round cheeks, and the same spontaneous friendly nature as well.

Jewels

Roche stopped off at his parents' place to look at the video of his famous Triple Crown in 1987 when, in a period of three months, he won the Giro d'Italia, Tour de France and the world title in Villach, Austria. Three major dates and he dominated them all - and with such class. Roche was the dictator of an

On the podium of the Giro d'Italia, flanked by Van der Velde and Millar.   *(Photo: AP)*

unforgettable campaign in which he refused to tolerate one ounce of resistance. In Italy, France and Austria, he was simply unbeatable.

On a sideboard are the three winner's jerseys of this legendary triple. Covered, from right to left: the pink jersey from the Giro d'Italia, the yellow from the Tour de France and the rainbow jersey of the world champion. Bonnie jealously protects these three prestigious garments of her former champion son. She dusts them down as if they were precious stones. Never will she allow them to lose their sparkle. They are valuable souvenirs, providing memories forever.

Poker

Speak of Roche's 1987 season and it's inevitable that you'll speak about Eddy Merckx, the only rider before Roche to have won the Triple Crown. "But that's as far as the comparison goes. I don't want in any way to be put on the same level as Merckx," says Roche. "It would be sacrilegious to compare my career with the Belgian champion's. The similarities are only valid in the case of this 1987 season. I once met Eddy at a bicycle exhibition and we spoke about our careers. We have a great amount of respect for each other. As men we have certain points in common, but we can't

World champion and winner of the Giro and Tour. *(Photo: Noël Truyers)*

be compared as cyclists. It wasn't for nothing that Eddy was nicknamed 'the Cannibal'. Everywhere and in every situation he was the strongest. Me, I had to figure out certain strategies and be more cunning to win. Of course, for me and other cyclists, it was all about pushing on the pedals harder than your rivals and riding just under your pain threshold. But I also reckon racing is about mistakes. You need to be able to win as you would in poker, to bluff and force the opposition into mistakes. When I won this way, the joy was intense. Like an actor who knocks everyone over in the stands, when I finish first I enjoy the ovation that is given to me just as much."

Undertaker

Roche revealed this tendency to bluff, his pronounced taste for playing poker, in great style on June 6, 1987. On this day, the Giro d'Italia had started its first decisive round and the Irishman, as cunning as a shark, was ready for the rendezvous. "On the third day of the race, Carrera won the team time trial, and I won the pink leader's jersey. But during the next time trial - an individual time trial - I had heavy legs. It was a bad day, as they say, which my team-mate Roberto Visentini profited from to take the jersey from me. I found myself in a bad situation which I absolutely wanted to get out of. What followed was a terrible psychological war between us. The Italian, Roberto, was also the son of an undertaker: sufficient for all of Italy to take him in their arms. I understood that I didn't have the slightest helping hand

from anyone. All the team was put at the service of Visentini, including the directeur-sportif. Only Eddy Schepers, my close friend and roommate, was still in my camp. There was no question of panicking. I felt strong enough to chase this win all alone."

Revenge

At this stage of the race Roche could have conformed to the ruling caused by the circumstances. He could have kept a lid on his temperament and accepted Visentini's leadership. As Greg LeMond did in 1985 on the Tour de France, when he let go of the reins to Bernard Hinault, he could have signed a pact of non-aggression with the Italian. Had he done this, he would have avoided so many problems and would have been warmly thanked by his employers. But the Irishman wasn't hearing from that ear. "I refused to cross my arms. I felt stronger than everyone and also I had a score to settle with Visentini. The year before, Roberto didn't believe in what was wrong with my knee. He openly accused me of play-acting, and I was obliged by the team administration to compete in the Barracchi Trophy with him. It hurt just to push on the pedals. He did all he could to humiliate me and looked for whatever way he could to drop me from his wheel; but I gritted my teeth. After the finish I went back to the hotel with a limp, so bad was the pain. That day I swore to take revenge on the Italian at the first occasion there was. That moment came. I had resolved to make up for my handicap. I was continuously in search of an opening. Finally, it came two days after Visentini's show of strength. In stage 14 from Lido di Jesolo and Sappada, I slipped into a counter-attack of a breakaway which included the future stage winner, Johan Van der Velde."

Attack

During this time, Visentini was soft pedalling at the back, surrounded by several team-mates and apparently unworried. Upon being told of what was happening, he sounded the alarm and just as quickly got back up to the front with his body guards. Too late: the bird had flown the coop. "I should admit that I had to be clever. It was out of the question to launch a clandestine attack against Visentini: that would not have been fair play and I would never allow myself to carry out that sort of conduct. Then again, nothing stopped me from protecting him by covering any attacks against the Italian; and to do that, such a situation needed to occur. When I sensed the occasion, I didn't hesitate. Also, I rode tempo to bridge the gap on Van der Velde and the other attackers.

"Behind, I could see the entire Carrera train riding tempo at the front of the peloton. Davide Boifava, the directeur-sportif of the team, was furious with me for what I had done, forcing me off the side of the road to put me out. "You have to wait for Visentini. That's an order,' he screamed. But I continued to ride, to enjoy my triumph. It gave me wings."

Spitting

It goes without saying that from that day on Roche endured troubled days. The public, lined along the side of the course, spat on him, insulted him, sprayed him with wine." All of Italy was sick of me, literally. The press pushed the issue to its maximum. I became a traitor, a hypocrite, a renegade.

"Before all this I had always been depicted to the Italian public as a nice lamb, and then I had the occasion to prove to everyone that I knew how to transform myself into a wolf with long teeth. The aggressive climate was amazing. Up until the finish of the race I was set on proving that I was well and easily the strongest.

"Amongst the team direction, the hot air finally subsided, especially when Visentini abandoned. With all his whining and complaining he wasted all his energy. He didn't accept my leadership, even when he revealed certain lapses in his condition. Clearly, he would never have lasted the distance and held onto his pink jersey to the end. For my part, I went on to win the final time trial. I was the strongest. This Giro d'Italia rightfully came to me."

In fact, the Irishman fended off Robert Millar, his closest rival, by 3 minutes and 40 seconds, and Erik Breukink by 4 minutes and 17 seconds.

Yellow fever

Theatrical production

Roche came out of the Giro d'Italia with his head full of ideas. Seeing his look of fire, it was clear the Irishman wanted more, that he felt stronger than ever before. "In fact, I didn't take the time to profit from my win in the Giro. With Eddy Schepers, my team-mate and only ally in Italy, we left the race almost immediately after the finish. I arrived back home at dawn, dead beat, my back like jelly after the long car trip. But there was no question of resting on my laurels. I jumped across the road to the bakery to buy some bread. We ate breakfast and at the end of the morning we went out training. The Tour was approaching quickly and I wanted to prove to everyone that I was the best in the team after my stand in the Giro.

Ambition

The young Roche went to contest a Tour de France as strange as it was exceptional. Open-eyed, overflowing with a rare sense of calm, he waited patiently for his hour before displaying his consuming ambition. On the stage to Villard de Lans, Roche put on the leader's yellow jersey for the first time. However, the next day, he inexplicably let Pedro Delgado take it over.

Then came the notorious 21st stage to La Plagne, one of the most incredible in the history of the Tour de France where Roche pulled off a physically mind-boggling exploit. "It was a terrible day. I rode off the front for 80km before Pedro Delgado caught me. The Spaniard was intelligent. He knew that to wipe me off his list of rivals he couldn't allow me to recover. So Pedro fired his first bullet straight away, attacking as soon as he caught me. It was impossible to follow him, but I had to limit the gap at any price if I was to reverse the order in the 38km time trial on the second last day. Physically, I couldn't beat Pedro who was a pure climber. I never had the capacity to fly up the mountains and take chunks of time out of others. Only something dramatic could save me. So off went the Spaniard, who's advantage started to climb."

Livid

Swept away by the events, Delgado felt as if he had wings, and the little native from Segovia increased his effort. "Behind, I tried to stay at my own rhythm. I couldn't let Delgado get more than a minute on me. Jf I did, it was lost. I knew that we were going to reach a sector of a

Irish, and proud to be so.
(Photo: Sergio Penazzo)

climb where I knew it was impossible to make a huge difference. At this point, when there was four kilometres to go before the summit, I gave everything I had to get back as much time as I could as quickly as possible. The element of surprise was on my side. Delgado couldn't be warned of what I was doing. When I came up alongside him, Pedro was livid. Morally, he took a real blow. The finish was so close, but he didn't have any psychological resources left to

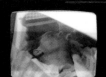
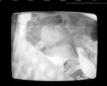

ambush me again. Finally, I only lost a few seconds to him. However, I was so wasted that I was taken to hospital. Just after the finish line, I fainted. I had gone so far past my limits. My batteries were flat. I was empty, exhausted. They had to give me oxygen with a barrage of cameras around me. I couldn't breath. I had blacked out."

Diversion

One hour later, back at the hospital where he had been admitted, Roche found his spirits back. Without knowing it, he was busy drafting the second act of a new development.

"I felt so tired. I felt nothing in the legs and I couldn't even eat, but that night I slept like an angel, without needing the slightest sleeping pill and I recovered as much as I could. The next day, at the start, apart from the usually heavy legs I didn't detect one worrying trace from what had happened the day before. Morally, in any case, I was well prepared. I really wanted to pull out something, and I had worked out my battle plan. I should add that I ingeniously hid my game. In fact, we were staying in the same hotel as Delgado and his team. Pedro was busy taking his breakfast when I came into the restaurant. My legs were so sore, but I immediately walked with apparent ease as if nothing was wrong. However, all my body was suffering. I put on a large smile and I saw Delgado change colour. Before this theatrical entrance the Spaniard was

With the green jersey, Jean-Paul Van Poppel.
(Photo: AP)

completely convinced that I was finished, and then, just like that, he sees me start the day as if I had just came back from holidays. His brewing confidence had just exploded.

Descent

That day, survivors in the Tour had to get to Morzine via passages over the Col de la Colombire and Joux Plane. Another apocalyptic stage, with a brutal heat wave leaving not the slightest shadow over the course for those 'slaves' of the road, desperate for water. "At the start, I wisely stayed back. I had bad legs and all my flexibility had gone. At the slightest change of rhythm, I was in pain and I seriously began to imagine the worst. But as time passed, I felt better and better. At

At the summit of La Plagne: exhausted and hospitalised. *(Photo: Luc Daelemans)*

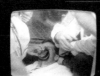

this point, I decided to get back to the front of the peloton and to control the race. I even tried to attack Delgado, but Pedro was very strong. Each time I accelerated he closed the gap with disconcerting ease. It was vital that I ride differently, that I change my tactics. Having climbed with the leaders to the summit of the Joux Plane, I decided to take the descent flat out. I released the breaks, descended into a seemingly bottomless pit by cutting the slightest corner and Delgado was K.O'd.

"He expected anything else, but that. At the finish I had pulled back 18 seconds and in the time trial on the second last day I took back the yellow jersey. I wasn't at my best for this decisive stage. The stakes were high and I was especially nervous. So much for the better that it was Jean-Francois Bernard who won. I started too slowly to have any hope of winning the stage. I was too afraid of having an accident. Finally, I recorded the second fastest time behind Jef. Delgado was a lot further back, and I was the happiest man in the world that day."

Minister

So, it was by 40 seconds over Delgado and 2 minutes and 13 seconds over Jean-Francois Bernard that Stephen Roche won the 1987 Tour de France - the very first time that the Grande Boucle had been won by an Irishman. Wearing his Irish cap, Roche finally let his jubilation free atop the podium. There, where Sean Kelly had systematically failed, Stephen Roche had succeeded with exceptional panache. What more would one need to light up conversation in the pubs around Ireland?

Upon receiving his last yellow jersey and the ovation of thousands of Irish fans who came to the Champs Elyses, Roche was flanked by the Irish Prime Minister. "At the start of the final stage I was still also leader of the points jersey; but to leave nothing to chance I allowed Jean Paul Van Poppel to go for it. By that I didn't have to contest the intermediate sprints. There was no question of taking the slightest risk so close to the end."

Left:
Determination written all over Roche's face.
(Photo: Graham Watson)

Right: The first Irishman to win the Tour.
(Photo: Luc Daelemans)

Rainbow

Zest for success

The Tour de France has handed down its verdict. The world championships in Villach, Austria, are already on the horizon. Roche ruled during the Tour of Italy and then France, but the world title was another matter altogether.

Roche began it with the sole plan of riding for Sean Kelly whose popularity had understandably been overshadowed by the exploits of his young compatriot. Kelly wanted at all price to balance the scales of his list of honours.

"After the Tour, the plan was that I would compete in a number of criteriums. Unfortunately, that was cut short. During the race at Grammont, I tore a muscle when there was a sudden change in rhythm on the most difficulty part of the circuit. The doctor ordered a complete stop. I rested for a week, then I did 11 criteriums one after the other to prepare myself for the world championship. I didn't have any choice. So, I went to the world titles feeling that I wasn't one hundred per cent. I gave myself hardly any chance of actually competing for the title. So, I was totally relaxed when I lined up for the start. In fact, I had nothing to lose and everything to win that day at Villach."

Option

True to his reputation, Roche had nonetheless thought out plan B. "More than anything, I had to play a bit of Russian roulette," he recalls, still as happy as he was then for having been able to succeed that time. "I heard that everyone opted for a 12-18 rear-block (gearing). So I asked a mechanic to put on a 13-20 which was more supple, which allowed me to spin more and save energy for the last hour of the race. In light of my limited preparation this option wasn't a wasted luxury. When the time came to engage a bigger gear nobody could follow me. God, how they must have cursed me. I knew that Sean Kelly had braked a bit behind me to help me get away. He found himself with Argentin. The Italian finally finished second and Juan Fernandez was third. Sean was as happy as if he had become world champion himself. He carried me to victory on his shoulders."

Cap

Straight after the finish, the two Irishmen gave each other a long hug. Wearing a new Irish cap, Roche hauled himself onto the podium at Villach and, overwhelmed with emotion, heard his national anthem. What seemed impossible a few hours earlier, had just become very real.

"Kelly was the leader. Before the world championship we agreed that it would be

Right:
World Champion. *(Photo: Sergio Penazzo)*

me who worked for him. Approaching the last kilometres I thought about Sean. In the front group there were a few dangerous names. For me, I had no choice. To win the title I had to reach the finish alone. In a sprint I didn't have a shadow of a chance against all these fast guys. It was at that moment that Teun Van Vliet attacked. I counter-attacked and Kelly stayed behind. It wasn't until this moment that I started to think of my own chances. In any case, for Sean it was finished. I was obliged to try my luck."

Reconnaissance

At the start of this incredible day, only one other person had won the Triple Crown. At Villach, Roche joined Eddy Merckx as the only riders to have won the Giro d'Italia, Tour de France and world championship in the same year. The man of the season confirmed his supremacy by taking the world title. "Sure, I had thought of that over the last kilometres. I knew what Merckx had done. But, well it was Merckx. As for equalling his performance, that was another matter. It was something that was less probable because I wasn't so good in the days before the race. The night before, my condition was a little bit better, but I still didn't have the slightest pretension of winning. Another thing was that I didn't think that the circuit would be selective enough. I gave riders like Eric Vander-aerden or Guido Bontempi more chance of winning. I was especially discouraged up until the Friday when Sean and I carried out a reconnaissance of the circuit. It was then that I realised that the sprinters wouldn't have a say, and that you had to be strong to stand out. I suddenly realised

The podium at Villach: Argentin, Roche and Fernandez.   *(Photo:Sergio Penazzo)*

Roche and his family immortalised. The price of being World Champion.   *(Photo: Noël Truyers)*

that I would have a card to play; especially if the heat wasn't there."

Wrestler

Unfortunately, Roche was never able to profit from his rainbow jersey. Once again falling victim to his knee problems, the Irishman was the major absentee from the peloton in the months that followed. "It was without a doubt the catastrophic consequence of this explosive season. Because of these health worries I didn't have the chance to confirm these wins. When I look back at the photo of Liège-Bastogne-Liège in 1988, it really annoys me. There I am, with six extra kilos. I look more like a wrestler than a cyclist. Always this confounded knee which has given me such a bad time. I was never the same man as a result, and the season I spent in the rainbow jersey was a real fiasco. By the end of winter, I had spent three months without touching my bike. The result: six kilos too many on the scales. It was a mortal blow for my condition. I was in despair for not being able to honour this jersey. I had never been one to hang back at the end of the peloton. When I started a race, it was always to show myself, to play a visible role. At that moment I forced myself to get back to my best. That was a mistake I shouldn't have made. I got worse rather than better."

Cross **roads**

Stephen Roche's career is not just full of happy stories. On the contrary, Roche would have been supported by an even more prestigious honour role had he not been so often hindered by knee problems. It was in 1984 that the first bad sign appeared, after a crash in the Paris Six Days track meeting. An operation was carried out to fix the problem, but it didn't provide the expected results.

Even worse, Roche was persuaded to go under the knife a second time in 1986. "I should never have agreed to this second operation; but I was overwhelmed with desperation when one doctor gave me his business card. It was a classic scenario: we are at the 36th cross-road and we think that we've put all our faith in someone. Then, later, we realise that we've taken the wrong direction.

"In fact, this operation was totally useless. That year, 1986, was not exactly pre-historic; but in the medical arena, we had progressed by a Century on the medical front. For a long time after that I was convinced that the injury worsened after 1987, during which time I did everything to win the Giro d'Italia, the Tour de France and world championship. However, at that time I was already in a pitiful condition. After the operation, I had to change my position on the bike: a change which was directly at the core of all my miseries."

Shop

Roche quickly threw himself into fulfilling one of his biggest dreams. "After my Triple Crown, Lydia and I did our winter accounts. I had earned a lot. In only a few more seasons, I would have reaped the rewards of my value and we would be secure for

Roche's crash on the Paris track was the start of numerous problems. *(Photo: AP)*

life. This became a preoccupation, so we invested some of my earnings into buying a house in Ireland and Lydia opened a shop in the centre of Dublin. At the start of 1988, I sold everything. I was discouraged mentally and physically. One more operation would have put me out."

Wohlfahrt-Müller

It was at this point that Roche met the notorious German doctor Wohlfahrt-Mller.

Roche and Kelly: profound friends.
(Photo: Graham Watson)

"At the start I didn't want to hear any talk of him. In my eyes there was no difference between him and his colleagues who had so far done nothing for my knee. "He is the doctor from the Bayern-Munchen football club," I was told. "He really has a golden touch."

"I let myself be convinced and when I went to his surgery I met Jean-Marie Pfaff, the goalkeeper of the Belgian football team. His patients included Boris Becker, Daley Thompson and Sören Lerby.

"With such customers he couldn't be doing

anything underhand. His approach to the problem was different to any that I had experienced before. He asked me to indicate exactly the area where my knee hurt. Confidently, he found it and localised exactly where the knee was infected, telling me exactly how he was going to fight it and how long the treatment would take."

Therapy

After the consultation, Roche made a decision. If he accepted the treatment by the well-known doctor, he was going to go through with it quickly. "Coming out of his surgery, I went to the very first supermarket and bought some pyjamas, underwear and personal effects. I didn't bring anything

with me. And we began the therapy straight away. There was no question of having another operation."

Injections

It took Roche another three seasons before he got back to top form again. In 1991, he won the Catalan Week and the Criterium International. The next year, he had to wait until the Tour of Spain before being able to really test himself. Then came his stage win in the Tour de France to La Bourbole, his sole success from 1992. "I experienced indescribable agony before I was able to be back up at my top form again. Every three weeks I had to go to Dr Wolfhart-Müller. Each time I was given 12 injections in the backbone to put fluid in the veterbrae. The quantity depended on the muscle contraction. This method built up the flexibility of the tendons. When they were compressed by the vertebrae, the pain became unbearable. When you had to climb over four mountain passes in one day, I hardly felt my left leg at all when I got off the bike. I never again found my old sensations in the time trial."

Roche also suffered from world champion's jinx.
(Photo: Luc Daelemans)

Adored then **disgraced**

Stephen Roche was a champion on the popularity stakes. He was admired by everyone, especially the women. Some of them even tried to say that the Irishman wasn't suited for the job of a cyclist: too nice, unable to put his fist down.

On certain occasions, Roche proved that he could be obstinate and would go as far as to seriously argue with those who got in his way. Some quarrels are stuck in the memory, notably against those who opposed members in his closely-knit entourage in most of the teams he rode for. It was the case at Carrera, Fagor, Histor and Tonton Tapis.

Valcke

Behind his teasing look and a natural spontaneity, the Irishman hides some strange characteristics. Roche has always defended his on-and-off fickleness. It's impossible to please everyone.

The fact is that when something doesn't go right, Patrick Valcke is always there. Roche and Valcke were very close. "But I protected him for too long and that was a mistake on my part. Patrick was a close friend. I owed him a lot. It was for this reason that I wanted him alongside me as my directeur-sportif. We even spent some of the rare moments of free time we had together. When I was doing rally driving, Patrick even spent some time as my co-driver. He then started to make mistakes, but as I was leader the criticisms fell on me.

A great time triallist.   *(Photo: Luc Daelemans)*

When our union ended, it was then that I discovered the true Patrick Valcke. He led a mighty public campaign against me in the press which was defamatory."

The trough

Gradually Roche approached the twighlight of his career, but in the 1991 Tour de France he wrote one of the most controversial chapters of his cycling. At the Dauphiné Libéré, he suffered from tendonitis. Only one remedy was possible - rest; but that was apparently out of the question. "I took opinions from a string of doctors. It was unanimous: it was impossible that I could get to my best form for the Tour." The Irishman still wanted to do his best, but on the second day he was eliminated from the Tour for being late for the start of the team time trial. "I was given the wrong start time," says Roche in his defence.

It was a story totally contradicted by Roger De

Left: Roche's season with Histor was a failure.
(Photo: Jan Van den Aeve)

Below: Champion of popularity
(Photo: Graham Watson)

Vlaeminck who was his directeur-sportif at the time. "It was deliberate. He was looking for a way out ," accused De Vlaeminck, known to everyone as 'Le Gitan' (the gypsy).

Eliminated

Roche still started the stage, lining up under the start line 14 minutes and 20 seconds late. Elimination was inevitable. "Why would I have done it deliberately? My wife took three week's holiday especially to watch the race, and I rented a mobile home for my parents to follow it. They came from Ireland to follow the stages in Brittany and Normandy. Do you think that I was capable of destroying all their dreams? If I really wanted to get out of it with all these honours, there were a thousand other ways to do it. In this scandal, I was treated like a criminal."

Divided brothers

Stephen Roche and Sean Kelly have always been close. Rivals in the peloton, yet loyal friends out of the race. However, the two Irishmen were eventually worlds apart when it came to their key objectives. Their selection of races always revealed different priorities. Kelly was a brilliant rider for the classics, the emperor of one day races. Roche was sublime in the Giro d'Italia, Tour de France and the world championship - races which Kelly no doubt dreamt about but could never finally claim as his.

Elegance

Hence, Roche and Kelly were very different. Kelly, a farmer's son, had his trademark of pure force and explosiveness. He had incredible strength. Roche, on the other hand, was very much a thoroughbred and moved with infinitely more elegance on the bike. Roche was almost at one with his machine. As gracious as a deer, he was also blessed with muscles bearing phenomenal strength.

Bed

The two Irishmen always kept their honest friendship alive, even when they were divided in their interests during their career by sponsors' demands. "We have always

Left: Kelly carries the champion on his shoulders. *(Photo: Graham Watson)*

Right: Rivals on opposite teams, but friends nonetheless. *(Photo: Graham Watson)*

respected our sponsors. Sean raced for his and I defended the interests of mine. I never had the chance to ride for the same team as his, but we have never tried to put a spanner into each others' spokes or anything. Sean had a great role to play in my world title win in Villach. It was him who motivated me before the race by convincing me that I could pull off the coup on such a course; and when Kelly gives his opinion on something you can be sure that he is reliable. His analysis really inspired me. I remember when we crossed the finish line in Austria, how he threw his hands in the air just as I had a few instants before. He was as happy about this title as I was; even though he made the world title one of his big goals for the year. A funny anecdote: on the night before the world title we slept in the same bed. The Irish federation reserved a double room, but instead of finding two beds for one person we found one double bed for two! That didn't stop us sleeping like angels. The bed was huge."

Idol

Roche and Kelly are not of the same age. But their starts were similar before their respective careers took different paths. "Sean started cycling four years before me, but I stopped one season before him. When I started, Sean was already well known. In fact, he was my idol. In a race, he was incredible. It was as if he never even felt the pedals. They say that riders like these only come every 25 years. For me, it was difficult to break through. I felt a bit rejected. Meanwhile, I fought on to be equal with Kelly."

Godmother

The popularity of the two cyclists was perceived differently by people in Ireland and on the Continent. In Ireland, Kelly was THE

indisputable star: a long way ahead of Roche. On the other hand, in France we were taken by the opposite phenomenon. Kelly was certainly appreciated, but nothing more. As a cyclist, Roche was always the preferred one in the eyes of the French public, and nothing really changed in this view. Roche is always in demand for public relations jobs on the Tour, or as a commentator for radio or television. "It's true that we do have different priorities and opposite attractions. At least that stops us from treading on each other's feet which only tightens our friendship. Sean's wife, Linda, is the godmother of my son Nicolas. Kelly and I, we trained together for years. We had one major point in common: we lived 100 per cent for cycling. As each new

Irish blood shared, but different characters.
(Photo: Graham Watson)

season approached, we packed our bags and we left for two months. We always did it that way and it was efficient."

Rookie

Their origins were just as different. Kelly's father was a farmer and Roche's was a Dublin milk man. Roche's childhood was one of a little city boy spoiled by his parents. "I was often criticised, and for the wrong reasons. It was as if everyone had put in doubt my strength of character. For many people, my Dubliner's heritage was a sign that I would never be mentally strong. 'Roche in France' as soon as he has ridden twice around the Arc de Triomphe he'll be back on the ferry for Ireland. This boy is nothing more than a milk man's rookie - too soft for this kind of job. I proved that all of

Two world classed riders.

that had no substance of truth, and without these knee problems."

Tie

Kelly is rarely seen in a suit and tie. He is a native of rural Ireland where he is isolated and surrounded by green pastures carrying livestock. In contrast, Roche is from an area full of yuppies where everything is spruced up with bricks.
"I could never live like Sean, and he would be unable to adapt to my environment. For many years he went to his brother's place while I preferred to count on nobody but myself. That said, I have utmost admiration for Kelly. When I see the ease he carries out certain things, with the flair that he is able to impress people, I could almost get a complex."

(Photo: Graham Watson)

Farewell

Every good thing comes to an end, even for elite sports stars. The retirement of Stephen Roche at the end of 1993 left a huge hole in the cycling world. It was almost as if the popularity of the Irishman had suddenly been recognised.

There were race organisers everywhere who wanted to hold farewell meetings in his honour. It was the case in France, then Ireland and finally in Belgium at the initiative of Opel Soers (his old rally driving sponsor). Many former Belgian professionals took part in a 'gentleman's race' in Neerwinden where Roche made his final appearance as a cyclist. As a farewell present, he was given the metal

wing of the Opel Corsa that he ran into a tree with in the Rally Condroz the year before!

La Bourbole

In fact, the former Tour de France winner could easily have spent one more year in the peloton to gradually prepare his body for its reconversion from cyclist to an everyday person. "It's true, I could have done it, but only for a question of money, and I didn't want it that way. I never raced for the sole goal of money. Before anything, it was for pleasure, the passion. I was already very happy to have gained some good results in

With his trusted domestique, Eddy Schepers.

(Photo: Rug)

my last year. I finished 13th in the Tour. I wanted to leave by the front door which I wouldn't have been able to do earlier because of my knee problems. That year, I promised myself to leave my mark for the last time on everyone's imagination. I especially wanted to win a stage - a challenge which required I train like a galley slave and look after myself meticulously. Luck brought a smile to my face that beautiful day in July, 1991, on the stage to La Bourbole. In the fog, I reached the summit alone after a fierce battle that lasted three hours. Taking my place atop the podium, I felt that the full cycle of my career was complete, that I had just completed the final part of my contract. That evening, as I slipped between the sheets, I felt that there was no longer any motivation."

A small world

Without a doubt Roche would have been able to physically continue racing. He still had more juice in the cranks, but his physical potential on the other hand had run dry. "Nine times out of ten it happens in the mind. Two years earlier I had already noticed the first signs of being mentally drained. People spoke to me about the preceding Tour and made predictions about the next. As for me, I felt more motivated about going to the supermarket with Lydia, going to a football match or going and supporting my son in a cross country running race. The old fire had gone, my priorities had changed. For 13 years I had lived egotistically in a small world. During all these years, I wasn't interested in anything or anyone else. Everything revolved around me. The time had come for a change in atmosphere, habits, life."

Decision

Roche didn't go back on his decision. He refused to take a new contract to concentrate

Goodbye Stephen ...   *(Photo: Rug)*

on other things in life. "At the beginning, it suited me. I was thrilled about it. In re-signing for one more year, I would have been able to bring home a handsome stash of money. Actually, I would normally have needed ten years to earn what was offered me at the time for 12 months. I hung onto this nostalgic idea until Paris-Nice the next year; in fact, up until I found myself in a VIP car and following Sean Kelly in full flight up a mountain. Sean had heavy legs, his eyes focused on the summit ahead. At this instant, I understood that I had made the right decision, that I stopped in time."

Memorial

Drawing up alongside a little place in Dundrum, Roche stops the car. Several passers-by look towards him. He responds with a wave and a large smile. "When I decided to stop, certain people believed that I had the right to a monument because of my win in the Giro d'Italia, the Tour de France and the world title in the same year. It's there, in front of you.

"The municipality didn't really back this project. To be honest, it didn't have any interest in erecting this memorial to Roche. Nor did I. In any case, it's the kind of thing for which I never really pushed for. I had it up to here with all their bureaucracy. It was here that my supporters intervened. They organised a fund in the corner of the bike shop. In a few days, it was full.

In the meantime the town wanted to contribute to its opening, but it was too late.

"The inscription on the stone is the work of a boy who was 12-years-old at the time. He had leukemia, a sickness which finally took him. This boy was my most loyal supporter."

Reserves

Roche gets back behind the wheel of his four wheel drive. He makes a call on his mobile phone. "It was Majorca," he says, after asking the caller to ring back a bit later. "I earned a good living on the bike,

In front of the monument in his name.

 (Photo: Noël Truyers)

but today I need to keep myself busy. If I was a bit richer I would have without a doubt lived until my eighties with what I had earned, but it's not my style. That said, I still have some savings. The money I won in the peloton is my down payment for my future. It's sleeping in my bank account. I don't touch it. I live off what I got from the two houses I sold."

Majorca

These days, the only Irish winner of the Tour spends his months organising cycling holidays and training camps for cyclo-tourists and club racers in Majorca. "That's why someone called me before. These trips are held 21 weeks every year. The concept started to be functional and profitable. At the beginning it's necessary to invest. Once on the camp, we work with trainers who look after the groups and accompany them during their rides, but the people also want to see me. Hence, I try to be at a camp for one weekend every fortnight for those who are there. I try to make sure that everyone is happy. We speak of the past, of my victory in the Tour de France, the

Invited to the presentation of the 1998 Tour with Jan Ullrich and Sean Kelly. *(Photo: AP)*

Giro d'Italia and the world titles. We speak about numerous subjects such as nutrition and self-care of a rider. It's a nice job."

Collection

Roche is still a big boy at heart. However, while under his exterior he appears a little naive, the man has also proven to be a leader in business. In 1987, exactly ten years after his legendary 'Triple Crown', he made 87 identical bikes in Italy. It was a unique collection: each bike numbered, with his name and three small jerseys - a yellow, pink and rainbow one - engraved on the frame. "It was an original idea that was profitable. All the bikes were quickly sold while I looked after the real launch of my own brand. For these models, I chose to sell them by mail. I took all the orders. I sent them to the factory with the exact dimensions, and from there they were made and sent to the clients. Business wasn't too bad, but it's been a long time

since I have profited from it."
Apart from that, Roche invested a lot of his time in the organisation of the Irish stages in the 1998 Tour de France. "I even offered my services to the Irish tourism office. I thought I would have made the perfect middle-man for them. It was impossible to miss this golden chance to present Ireland as a holiday location to the world. It was a very restless period. You had to think of everything."

Eternity

Since then Roche has returned to business. In the Tour, he continued to work in public relations. Without a doubt he will continue to do so for a good while longer. Roche will be 47 during the 20th anniversary of his 'Triple crown' in 1987. He will probably have grown a few extra grey hairs, but his legendary spontaneity to life won't have changed."

The pink jersey ... a veritable giant.

(Photo: Noël Truyers)

Visitors' book
Stephen Roche

Born: Dublin, 28/11/59

1982: Peugeot
0 wins
Other results: Nice-Alassio (5th), Tour du Haut Var (9th), Tour of Corsica (6th),
Paris-Nice (6th), Midi-Pyrénées (4th), Liège-Bastogne-Liège (9th), Amstel Gold
Race (2nd), Four Days of Dunkirk (3rd), World Championship (32nd), Blois-Chaville
(18th), Tour of Lombardy (16th), Barracchi Trophy (3rd).

1983: Peugeot
5 wins: Tour of Romandy (overall classification), Grand Prix de Wallonie, Paris-
Bourges (stage 1 and overall), Etoile des Espoirs (overall).
Other results: Tour Méditérranéan (4th), Tour du Haut Var (2nd), Criterium
International (5th), Midi-Pyrénées (3rd), Paris-Roubaix (20th), Liège-Bastogne-Liège
(24th), Amstel Gold Race (20th), Grand Prix Frankfurt (17th), Midi Libre (5th), Tour
de France (13th), Clasico San Sebastian (7th), Grand Prix Plouay (3rd), World
Championship (3rd), Grenoble (2nd), Isbergues (10th), Grand Prix des Nations (5th),
Blois-Chaville (7th), Tour of Lombardy (18th).

1984: Peugeot
4 wins: Nice-Alassio, Paris-Nice (stage 6), Tour of Romandy, Subida Arrate.
Other results: Tour Méditérranéan (2nd), Tour du Haut-Var (4th), Kuurne-Brussels-
Kuurne (6th), Paris-Nice (2nd), Milan-San Remo (28th), Criterium International (3rd),
Ghent-Wevelgem (16th), Paris-Roubaix (21st), Amstel Gold Race (19th), Grand Prix
Frankfurt (32nd), Tour de L'Oise (2nd), Dauphiné Libéré (6th), Tour de France (25th),
Fourmies (15th), Grand Prix des Nations (3rd), Baracchi Trophy (6th), Blois-Chaville
(18th), Tour of Lombardy (5th).

1985: La Redoute
13 wins: Paris-Nice (stage 7b), Criterium International (stage 2 and overall), Midi-
Pyrénées (stage 1 and overall), Dauphiné Libéré (prologue and stage 9), Tour de
France (stage 18), Bol d'Or, Tour of Ireland (stages 3 and 4), Les Ormes, Laudeac.

Other results: Tour Méditérréanéen (3rd), Cannes (4th), Tour du Haut Var (5th), Paris-Nice (2nd), Milan-San Remo (51st), Flèche Wallonne (20th), Liège-Bastogne-Liège (3rd), Amstel Gold Race (11th), Dauphiné Libéré (20th), Midi Libre (7th), Tour de France (3rd), World Championship (7th), Toulouse (2nd), Grand Prix Eddy Merckx (5th).

1986: Carrera
0 wins
Other results: Tour de France (48th), Baracchi Trophy (7th).

1987: Carrera
15 wins: Tour de France (stage 10 and overall), Tour of Italy (stages 1 and 22 and overall), World Championship, Tour de Valence (stage 3 and overall), Paris-Nice (stage 8), Tour of Romandy (stages 5a and b), Kortenhoef, Dublin, Aalsmeer.
Other results: Morvedre (2nd), Puig (5th), Pantalica (5th), Paterno (4th), Noto (3rd), Paris-Nice (4th), Milan-San Remo (74th), Criterium International (2nd), Tour of the Basque Country (12th), Flèche Wallonne (4th), Liège-Bastogne-Liège (2nd), Henninger Turm (4th), Bavel (2nd), Stiphout (4th), Chaom (2nd), Scherpenheuvel (3rd), Grammont (2nd), Tour of Ireland (2nd).

1988: Fagor
0 wins
Other results: Chaumol (4th), Tour of Great Britain (6th), World Championship (76th), Tour of Ireland (80th).

1989: Fagor
4 wins: Paris-Nice (stage 7b), Tour of the Basque Country (stage 5b and overall), Four Days of Dunkirk (stage 3).
Other results: Paris-Nice (2nd), Criterium International (3rd), Tour of Flanders (30th), Liège-Bastogne-Liège (33rd), Amstel Gold Race (38th), Four days of Dunkirk (3rd), Tour of Italy (9th), Tour of Ireland (22nd).

1990: Histor
2 wins: Four days of Dunkirk, Calais
Other results: Paris-Nice (2nd), Catalan Week (7th), Criterium International (6th), Tour of the Basque Country (6th), Flèche Wallonne (6th), Liège-Bastogne-Liège (16th), Amstel Gold Race (39th), Tour de L'Oise (21st), Dauphiné Libéré (7th), Midi Libre (5th), Tour de France (44th), Wincanton Classic (46th), Tour of Great Britain (14th).

1991: Tonton Tapis
3 wins: Catalan Week, Criterium International, Brioude
Other results: Sicilian Week (9th), Paris-Nice (4th), Tour of the Basque Country
(7th), Flèche Wallonne (16th), Liège-Bastogne-Liège (8th), Amstel Gold Race
(72nd), Wincanton Classic (34th), Paris-Tours (109th).

1992: Carrera
1 win: Tour de France (stage 16)
Other results: Tirreno Adriatico (8th), Milan-San Remo (35th), Catalan Week (7th),
Criterium International (7th), Tour of the Basque Country (6th), Flèche Wallonne
(12th), Liège-Bastogne-Liège (14th), Tour of Spain (14th), Tour de France (9th), La
Bataille (5th), Chaumeil (3rd), Zurich (58th), Tour of Venis (12th), World
Championship (23rd), Vouneuil (2nd), Tour of Ireland (5th), Paris-Tours (50th), Tour
of Pimont (2nd), Tour of Lombardy (18th), Montjuich (7th).

1993: Carrera
0 wins
Other results: Tour of Italy (9th), Milan-San Remo (126th), Liège-Bastogne-Liège
(24th), Amstel Gold Race (46th), Tour of Romandy (13th), Tour of Tuscany (9th),
Tour de France (13th).

47

This book, 'Stephen Roche' is the third of the Cycloscoop series in which Noël Truyers looks at the stars of the international peloton. It follows those already published on Miguel Indurain and Sean Kelly and is followed by portraits on Briek Schotte, Jan Raas and Herman Vanspringel.

Colophon

Published by Eecloonaar
Industrielaan 44
9900 - Eeklo, Belgium
Tel: ++ (32) 0 9377 1182
Fax: ++ (32) 0 9378 1234
Internet: www.eecloonaar.be

Author: Noël Truyers

Designed by: Eecloonaar Printers.
Industrielaan 44 - 9900 Eeklo

Binding: Proost, Turnhout

Translation: Rupert Guinness

Ook beschikbaar in het Nederlands

ISBN 90-74128-26-2
Legal deposit: D/1998/5813/12
C 1999 Editions Eecloonaar

Photos and illustrations

Photo have been made available to us from the archives of AP, Bettoni, Luc Daelmans, Frank Quinn, Sergio Penazzo, RUG, Noël Truyers, Graham Watson, Jos Vanhamel. Results: Harry Van den Bremt. In the case where publication of photos can't be made by an official request to the photographer because of unknown origins, the author can contact the publisher.